Black Rhinos

By Julie Haydon

Illustrations by Celina Korcak

Contents

Why Black Rhinos Are Endangered

The black rhinoceros is in danger of dying out.

In the 1960s, there were more than 100,000 black rhinos alive in Africa.

Africa

Today, there are fewer than 3,800 black rhinos.

There are many reasons why black rhinos are in danger of dying out.

Black rhinos have two horns on their snouts. Some black rhinos are killed for their horns.

The horns are used in some medicines and to make knife handles.

This knife handle is made from black rhino horn.

Today, people live in many places
where black rhinos once lived.
People have cleared the land to build homes
and start farms.

It is difficult for black rhinos to find food
on land that has been cleared.

It is also difficult for black rhinos
to hide from people
who might want to kill them
on cleared land.

Many black rhinos now live in national parks.
The workers at national parks
protect the black rhinos from hunters.
They make sure the black rhinos
have enough food to eat.

Looking for Blossom

Kam drove the jeep carefully
over the African grassland.
His friend, Jeff, was beside him.
Jeff was looking through binoculars,
slowly searching the grassland for rhinos.

"Can you see Blossom?" Kam asked.

"There's no sign of her," replied Jeff.

Kam and Jeff worked as rangers
for the national park,
and Blossom was a black rhino
that lived in the park.

Nobody had seen Blossom for several weeks,
and everyone was worried about her.

"Maybe we should go on foot from here,
and try to find her tracks?" said Jeff.

Kam parked the jeep
and the two men climbed out.

They slung packs onto their backs
and set off.

"Look," cried Jeff, suddenly,
and pointed to the ground.
"These are fresh rhino tracks."

"Let's hope they are Blossom's," Kam said. "And let's hope no poachers have seen them. They'd kill her for her horns."

Quietly, Kam and Jeff followed the tracks.

They stopped
when they saw large grey shapes
in the distance.
Blossom was standing
in front of an overhanging tree
and something else was just behind it.

"Blossom's had a calf," Jeff said.
"No wonder she wanted to be alone."